Rumours of Paradise/
Rumours of War

George Amabile

M&S

Canadian Cataloguing in Publication Data
Amabile, George, 1936-
Rumours of paradise/rumours of war

Poems.
ISBN 0-7710-0736-1

I. Title.

PS8551.M32R8 1995   C811'.54   C95-930121-6
PR9199.3.A53R8 1995

The publishers acknowledge the support of the Canada Council and
the Ontario Arts Council for their publishing program.

Typesetting by M&S, Toronto
Printed and bound in Canada on acid-free paper.

McClelland & Stewart Inc.
The Canadian Publishers
481 University Avenue
Toronto, Ontario
M5G 2E9

1 2 3 4 5   99 98 97 96 95

RUMOURS OF PARADISE/
RUMOURS OF WAR

"Talk is cheap."
                    —*Anonymous*

SMALL TALK

TABLE TALK

SHOP TALK

SMALL TALK

FINDING A SYNTAX FOR BLUE PERFUME

Just before dawn
distilled
enigmas (tiny bells
of starlight?) open
at the top of this leafy cave
in the hedge I sometimes come to
when my head hurts and I can't
think anymore.
           In here
a raw but austere
fragrance clears
my head (the way a window
will suddenly melt
into distance when the lights go off
and the night is an infinite shimmer of worlds . . .

EXILE

The moon
is a bone
face, charged
with emergency
and patience
adrift in the blue
distance
between stars
and the small fires of home.

I turn into the back lane behind the hotel,
aim myself at the dented, aluminum-skinned
door. Light from a buzzing fixture
glazes the wet cement, lays
a steady gloss over puddles,
ricochets from a broken glass.

I've been here before, two or three times
a week for sixteen years, feeding
wrinkled bills under the grate
swinging my box of Blue back through the night.

At the last intersection, leaves
blow up and rush
down the wide street
like a spontaneous migration
and suddenly I'm overcome
by the bearable lightness of being
alone with the sagging eaves
and rain pipes of neglected houses,
their crooked rooms lit like Hallowe'en
pumpkins, and above them, the moon
flaring or dim behind swift clouds
the pavement uneven,
the future erased with every step.

Mystery gives way
to belief and belief
gives way to knowledge
and the small teeth
of the mind grind
on, though safety
is nothing more than time
disguised as a clock.

The season fades, revives
old loves, old failures
that hover in fragrant shadows
on cool wings, as we cruise
toward what we're told
are more controlled adventures.

Perhaps our thoughts
are only ghostly paradigms
of need. On the street
fistfuls of dusty noise
assail them. We invent
revised geographies
but when we stop
to breathe, a glimpse
of everything at once melts
their sensitive connections.

Fog swirls in the park, erasing
the trees, the granite horsemen.

KILL

Body
of water, brackish, dilute
ocean, adulterate
and calm among cattails, faintly
stagnant in the nose like a vintage
that died years ago in the basement
of an abandoned farm.

After the first release
of breath from locked muscles in the throat,
after a short emptiness
in which the voice enters and fills
the soft intricate resonant caves of the skull,
there is this lovely touch of tongue-tip to palate
just at the edge where flesh gives way to bone.

The rest is history.

CANDLE END: RUSSIA, 1917

The wick
glows like an incandescent
woman with a blue cape
that flutters as she turns
in the darkness of a deserted square.

The way
we talk love
is a force
field that goes
on on
its own below
us under
the appearances
of home
town dreams
we tumble into
or heavily
through with
or without
others.

        But love
        can't disguise
        itself
        underfoot like rain
        -bow quick
        sand hell
        no it just
        sings
        inside with
        or without
        others.

the truth, we tense
up, focusing, like a glass
eye, the mind, the reaches
of being into a tight
glare. If we loved
this way, we'd find each other
distant as the stars . . .

Trying to say
straight words only
we squeeze the branching lines
of blood, of centuries
into a flat
maxim, but even truth
has its changes
like scarves of light kissing the nerves.

We answer with names,
with theories. This
is the flux we inhabit.
It cannot be thought
out, it's what we are.

The way is concealed
        and has no name.

You love the map
        more than the journey.

Your failure to listen
        has left you nothing to say.

Expect the inevitable
        decay of good intentions.

Soon, unacknowledged appetites
        will break out in a rash of lies.

You will make new friends
        who thrive on hostile gossip.

No matter how hard you try
        to hide, Money will find you.

You are the rich
        father you killed in a dream.

TABLE TALK

YOU ARE WHAT YOU EAT

How cozy.
I don't think so.
I think we are what eats
us – an old friend's invisible
morning-after animals
nibbling at his considerable
intelligence, making his hands shake
at the snooker table. Isn't that more
à cout de la vie and worth
our time than the snotty face
in a margarine ad whose logic would make you
a broccoli spear or a sweet
pepper?

Once
in a serene
environment, I sat
in the shadow of a Maguey plant,
nursing a nearly empty bottle
of mescal and became aware
that there was an organized movement
down in the dark seams
of my workpants. Ants
were digging out and transporting
little forgotten treasures of gold
corn meal and such. They are so
bourgeois, you know, they probably don't
know how to just hang out, they probably have to
get something done even when they're away

15

on vacation. Anyhow, I liked looking down
at their geography because it made me feel
like a god or at least a giant, and I stayed
there in the shade watching them stagger
under heroic loads, their stuttering
caravans chaining into the limitless daze
of a desert/ed afternoon until
my lover arrived in a taxi. We had planned
to meet in town but I was not in good control
of my time and she had to shout
from the road, which I resented.
Nevertheless, it was the first day
of her vacation and no one seemed interested
in sampling her random lust but me so we did
what you can easily imagine. I remember lying
on my back, watching the fan turn
slowly through the heavy air, and thinking
about a perhaps gin and tonic while she worked
herself up to an expertly managed
climax but still remained unsatisfied because
suppose someone had observed this failure
to finish together like a dance team on Reach for the Stars.
"What's wrong," she said. "What's eating you?"
I looked out the window. Gulls
were buzzing the fuzz at the edge of the sand.
I scratched around but couldn't quite feel
where the itch was coming from, though by then
I could see the truth in her face. Whatever it was
that was eating me, I had become it. Seaweed
maybe, blessed with insect intelligence? I knew
right then I had to fight back. We got dressed
and she piggy-backed me down to the outdoor cafe
where I drank a couple of Carta Claras
and forced down little pieces of turtle steak
until my blood reversed
itself and I had to go swim in the channel.

Sometimes I think
hunger takes us close
to the light.

I often tell myself
remember to love
what you eat

(not for the nervous edge it calms as a lullaby calms an anxious
child before sleep. Not for the sense of power either. Or for the
reassurance provided by traditional cuisines. Or even for the
chemistry that changes diverse corpses into the same old you,
holed up in a circle of growing resentment, mooning around
for decades twice a day, routinely stunned by new ideas. But
because you share the history of Auks and Whales and
Redwoods; because you can hear the creak of your neckbones
echo through sub/terranean skull caves; because you feel
reborn when friendly disasters open windows in the film of
boredom that forms over the objects of your everyday world;
because when you love what becomes you, your body's habitual
misgivings can relax into simple tasks – planting seeds,
bringing in wood for the fire, scattering crumbs over clean
snow for the birds.)

Out in the kitchen, the cucumber and chicken-heart
ragù is bubbling quietly as a mud flat
and I'm in the den, immersed in exotic travel
brochures, trying to make myself see what
it might be like to walk in the sun through the start
-ling ruins of Mexico. Would it help me unravel
the primitive glitches that nest in my everyday brain?
Go stir the pot. Sniff it. Think up a name.

At supper, chambered muscles lie in state,
blurred by the sheet-lightning of brandy flambée,
like a boatload of organs ripped from the sawed rib-cage
by priests who knew their victims would scream and wake
in the house of the sun. Their books were knotted skeins
of hemp . . . "It's new," I say. "Linguine Azteca."

When they talk that way
they are like sailboats
trying to outrun each other
but limited by the wind
that flutters above this tidy cove
whose hillsides harbour
exquisite but little known vintages
in the cellars of obscure estates
where countless generations
of spiders have prepared
exactly the right grey
draperies, and they tack
smartly, avoiding direct
expression, thinking
themselves companionable
(neither too forward nor shy)
as they reaffirm the edge
of their importance
though they seem only to sip
and converse, careful not to raise
their voices unnecessarily, but savouring
words like *madras* and *pentimento*
while cheerfully discovering happiness to be
a fiction useful among the poor,
and noticing, too, how the tallest palms
resemble the brushwork of a Japanese master
on a broad band of flame-coloured silk, there
in the sunset just out of reach.

I'm watching flames lick
and blacken and eat
soft wood, fringed
with intimate curls
of birch bark. I'm discovering
that happiness is not a result.

And as I discover this I'm interrupted.
A voice on the answering machine
is getting testy. I know you're in there,
you bastard, pick up the phone!

I sip my Rémy Martin.

I can afford to burn
expensive fuel. And yet
I will soon have to think
about dinner, friends
invited long ago, a brief
enthusiasm like the spurt
of a match, an appetite
for more good times, on a far
-off evening which is now.

Maybe I could just send out
telepathic disclaimers. Who,
after all, could blame me
for choosing to travel incognito
through the lit vicissitudes
of oxygen and cellulose whose laws
are more elegant and dependable
than those that seem to dance around
a punch bowl? Don't get me wrong,

I know there will be serious talk,
strokes, outrageous news – things
we've come to rely on.
For now, though, I declare
this moment a ritual, a secret
pact with nothing
any of us would ever admit we crave.

1

It was Thanksgiving.
Annette's younger sister, Marlene,
and her boyfriend, Blaine,
were blanching and freezing
the last of the garden. Then George
dropped by to finish painting the house
again, and a full-fledged turkey
dinner came together out of the blue
(or out of the grey, if you want
a weather report). We lifted our wine
and the glasses, clicking and pinging,
made a sensitive music
like windchimes or distant bells.

2

It was a grey afternoon.
I'd been trying to write
a new poem but had no momentum.

I took the Butterball's body cage
from the fridge. Listing
badly and beached in sand
-coloured muck it looked
like something the sea
had returned, scraps
of discoloured sailcloth draped
over spars and ribs . . .

3

While the stock simmered
I sat in my study and read
through a stack of draughts
I'd written over the years.
It was depressing, but now
and again phrases, lines,
would brighten and ring
a little, like brass
windchimes or distant bells.

4

When I had drained the broth
and covered it and placed it
in the freezer (later, I'd skim
the lid of pale yellow fat)
I started to carry the sieve
to the trash when I noticed
among the struts
of the wings, among the knuckles
and leg stems and skin, a few
choice bits which I culled
for the soup, and there
was the shape of my new poem
and the title of this one.

SHOP TALK

PROCESS WRITER AT WORK

for Bob Kroetsch

1

How to begin. What is
the structure about/within
which abundance verifies
its ghost? A foreground
making up (for)
everything it leaves
out or unsaid. And once
you have the form, the direction, how
to escape the invisible bell
jar, the hypo
-thesis, airless
acid nipping the tips
of thought? Think
away from it, then
fuck, look at that, it's
gone. Now
you can begin and have

begun: when
I was a child:
a door opens
into immensity. All
those memories drifting
under the chop, the brisk
wind, stress

patterns even in stainless
contemplation.
                          Back then
I took my troubles, one
by one and one
day at a time,
to a small room
the lack of nourishment
had hollowed out
in a hedge. Dusty
and unpromising. A problem
for gardeners: traumatic
embolism, dead
zone in the profusion
intelligence planted
and pruned, a shadow
dome of failure in the green
screen between
someone's right
to privacy and the public
sidewalk. What happened
there in that sun-flecked, breezy
vacancy where brittle
tips poked me and broke
and fell into my shirt I can re/
member, I can in/
vent. But what went
on will not go
on again. Now it's a
problem in aesthetics:
background endlessly re/
novated by the structure
no one has to begin
with. This
is the open
ending of a world.

2

Tears. The stress
of day by day
living hand
-me-down dreams
(trying to pump
them up again
in the fifties,
the family
driving a new
used car to the sea)
left me
empty and fed
up with their hunger, those
who missed the good old
war, sick
of their need
for me to grow up
in the space death
made by erasing
millions of lives
millions of dollars
and chances too and I ran
away to sit in my hole
in the hedge
where all day long
I wanted to give
my sadness to somebody else.

Okay, but whose
pain is it now
that I've written
this? Whose grief surrounds
the child I pretend
to re/member, re/

inventing his/story
his desolate cave
in the hedge the years
have held
on to because
what else *was* there
then, for a child
in the wake
of the greatest of wars?

1

No one knows how it starts. Or when.
Maybe it's the first awareness
of pleasure. Or need. A print
we bury deep that cultivates an aesthetic
hunger . . .
                    Later, we'll discover
media: Mud. A hollow stem
with insect holes. A tin pot, a guitar.

Now and then, a shock wave
of percussive light warms as it unfolds
patterns we recognize but have not
lived. We go home to our strings,
our wheels, our labours. The feel
of it is in our heads, a shape
that satisfies vacancy. But it's not
in our hands, our fingers, though we keep
some ghostly echo for a while, practising
technique (which is best understood
by its absence). Never
mind. Begin
again. Listen.
                    One day it might be raining,
there's nothing to do in the park,
so you pick up your flute, your brush, your notebook
and let yourself wait, staying
out of the way until it's done
and gone.
                    A week, a month, sometimes
years later you think of it
fondly and it returns, like a hawk
or a dove and the journey begins.

2

Blather and swim
blather
and swim and swim
and blather
until you arrive
nowhere
you can ever have
imagined.

3

Robert Frost,
I tell you it's harder to play
tennis with the net
down. You have to
use your whole
mind, you have to love
the soul of the game
more than personal glory.

4

There is no style
or voice or applied
theory, there is only
what happens
when alignment erases
everything but
silence: fire
from within, then,
is the language
the substance, the song.

5

Method is the shadow
-analysis nostalgia
swears by. Once, candlelight
and wine in the cold
storage room under sounds
of wind in the pines
and fountains of Rome condensed
my homesick weariness
into words. Now, every sentence
evaporates memories, goes on
alone in the dark like an organ
of smell at the end of a fuse.

Where this particular poem
or its incompatible
neighbour comes from and how
they begin or arrive or decay
in the mind, on the page, in a book
on the shelf of a lifelong friend
is mysterious still. Nothing
too is shapely and fragrant. The steps
we invented once to climb
out of grief collapse
underfoot, the places,
the landmarks, the sure-minded
rhymes, the rhythms, oh
it won't come back
again, that iron animal, that
machine. Even the "act
of the mind" cannot distinguish
itself from the desert
places, the flood of dark
laughter, the whisk
of a snowflake in dead

leaves. What shall we make
and for whom and for how
long? Is a better poem
the same as a better
weapon? What is it
for, if not money
or money's ghost, prestige?
And should we go back
to the ways of ancient Greece
where genius could still make
an honest living
praising the King?

6

Work the blue scales
from the irises
of muse after muse
until their eyes
come on, come on, come on, come on
shining with white
light, once
and for all.

7

If the best you can say to yourself
when you're dying is, well,
I spent most of my time
making oddly beautiful structures
out of words, texts
that can never be marketed
as programs for Utopia,
cures for the infinite symptoms of stress,

or even as the shoots of a new religion;
if all you can say is, while I was wasting
time there were those who couldn't stop
spilling
milk, beans, classified secrets, innocent blood;

and if
when you begin to feel
okay about those virtues
of omission, the air hums
and blisters and dead relatives
turn their backs on you because
they'd hoped you could have left more of an echo,
more of a blaze in which their names might have shone,

how will you resign yourself
to your place in the history of doubt,
puttering, turning the limited syllables over
and over, discovering
to yourself in a lost voice how ". . . this
is not quite true, that's not exact
-ly right . . .," while pelicans
cruise on extended wings
back and forth across invisible borders?

to Hart Crane

> *... my faith*
> *toward something far*
> *now farther than ever away.*

• *New Thresholds, New Anatomies!*

So. Do those pages
you agonized for decades over
still contribute
white rings of tumult
to workshops and seminars,
to the breeze that blows in the mind
through all transilient models
of the real? *Only*
in darkness is thy shadow
clear. You were legendary
among the few. I took
that sparse tribe for the world,
but who ever heard of you
in the streets of the Windy City
or the Art Deco playpens of L. A.
Even your spectacular death
went by with hardly a ripple.
Still, when I read them,
your words leap
and burn.

• *O Dionysus*

Tipple. Sip. Foam
burgeons in the ballooned
glass, and bubbles rise
mindless as instinct
from a lucent but impervious
base. Night life
dwindles, *its fiery*
parcels all undone,
into steamy morning
traffic that revs
and crawls over the classical
bridges of the city. Crowds
materialize on the margins
of the day, dressed
to kill, herded by abstract
considerations, feeding
and feuding under the strut
of public clocks. I lean
toward hibernation at this window
under death-coloured leaves, under boughs
blackened by night
-long rain. *Is what I feel*
that patience that is
armour and that shields
love from despair – when love
foresees the end? You
entered the broken world,
burned with an impractical desire
to sing it whole again, then took
your incandescent centre back
to the sea. How long did it take
the terrible puppet to grow
still after the wake
of the ship had foamed and sighed?

- *The Gymnast of Inertia*

Maybe the lesson
of your unrequited
genius is not to expect
applause. Oh
*chimney-sooted heart
of man,* the stars are *dead
sands flashing. Already
snow submerges an iron year.*

Knowledge and belief
are *apparitional
as sails that cross*
in the mind. Words
and formulas unfold
across the page like spilt
milk, like water
under the complex bridges
of memory. Insights
flash from the white
ennui of memos, the trivial
compulsions of the law.

Is love *a burnt
match skating in a urinal?
When wine redeems the sight*
what do we see? Once, I drove
all night, under the cold
stars, wrapped
in the turbulence of open windows
and I spilled my grief to the dark
pine-scented earth, marvelling
how my voice, or any voice,
will strive in a whirlwind
toward unpredictable resonance

toward *the silken, skilled
transmemberment of song.*

· *Brazen Hypnotics*

We have burrowed and held on
to heavy metal and immense
dust, believing that amplitude
is grandeur, only to falter
under uncountable stars.

*Because we are
usurpers and chagrined*
we insist on our god
-given right to sell
what no one owns.

And the push goes on –
blind energy and endless expertise.
We are told and believe
that the mind is a switchboard,
that all the valences portend
a mathematics empty of desire.

· *The Calyx of Death's Bounty*

Sometimes when I walk
by the sea I think
how what the water made
of you rose, molecule
by molecule, into thin
rain, and the word you spent
weeks tracking down
explodes from the tips of waves:

spindrift, over stones,
over stunted trees, and its ghost
collects in my hair
or like beads of cold
sweat in my eye
hollows. Still, this is no
elegy but a gratitude. You
heaped the impasse high
with choir. Your *terraced echoes*
guide us as we build
and fail, and build again.

In the street, the roar
of a bus heaves, fades
to a hiss, then silence
and the *hopeful plasm*
of your voice revives
a *reconcilement of remotest mind,*
a bridge from the grave
of water then, *fiery blossoms*
and wild prefigurations of *Cathay.*

April 27, 1982

BRIDGE RIFF

for John Mackenzie

It's almost new
this metal railing
wet after a hard
rain. I set my elbows
down into cold sweat
and look upriver.

A breeze I can't feel yet fans out
from its nesting place among fresh leaves,
thrumming a stretch of dull water,
raising a bright hatch like insect wings

and the first cars,
spotless after their Sunday bath,
begin to nose out of the side streets,
their sealed beams brisk
and unnecessary
under the brightening sky,
which has already washed
faint cloud shadows
over those the still-burning street
-lamps make
out of boughs, birds,
and me,
and there is this

lightness

as though the soft gates of the body
had begun to exchange personal history
with the drift of river time

like the mix of matched guitars,
the raw voice of a harp,
words pulled out of memory, muscle, and sweat,
Kimberly's big eyes fluttering shut,
her slender legs curled in a sleeping bag,
the delicate snore that flared her nostrils
almost in 4/4 time,
like the crickets,
like the rain that shook the windows,
like the fridge in the kitchen
kicking in, like the embers
ticking, under a crust
of ash . . .

On the river
tiny wings dissolve
into a watercolour:
violet-edged skyline
dotted with bright green
impressionist trees.

   My fingertips burn

      on the strings. The music
      starts again. The wine
      got crisper as it chilled
      in its wash of melting ice.
      Then there was brandy
      and smoke wasting away
      in the air, its buzz
      already fading from the blood
      which cleans itself
      incessantly like a cat . . .

When I hit the street
for the long walk back,
it was night. Now

it's morning. The bridge
trembles under my feet
as traffic rumbles over the Red
into a trapped stampede.

    . . . always

        after lots of nothing much
        there is this unpredictable
        rightness, like the breeze

that starts again and blows
our urban renaissance

    apart like a puzzle
    only stillness has the heart
    to heal,
    and I can't tell

        whether we sang better
        on brandy or wine
        or water cold from the tap,

        and I don't know why I think

of Patrick in Swift Current,
the stone he brought
home like a lost pet
and the stone's lichen
exactly the colour of glacial till

but white at the edges
like a drying lake
seen from the top of a mountain,
the sprinkle of rain
he shook from his own hands four times
a year, and the way
he'd stand and observe it
patiently, open-minded
as the sky,

    and yes, it's outrageous
    to indulge in these
    unprofitable pastimes
    while the living
    we should be making starves
    and the banks

        of the river fail,
        crumbling
        into little whirlpools

as the city smokes and breaks
new ground.

It's Monday but the moon is thin,
a memory trace

            over the brawling world.

Having a beer
    at The Acropolis
   lounge on Sherbrook
in Winnipeg, but really

  I'm crossing a bridge

    the water-top
    undulates flaked adobe, thunder
    -heads and wealthy
    azure
           (I've never been
    here before but I like
    the name, the music
    drifting from an open window
    under a boiling sky, the way
    time deepens
             (afternoon
    shadows in the broken streets
    where everything I see
    as my life is far
               away (hills
      the colour of wood smoke,
      heat waves melting
      the trees over terra cotta roofs,
      charcoal and roast goat
        in the wind
        that comes off the desert,
        steady and close
        as a blow dryer
        but already losing
        its fever to the first
        few stars, heartbeat

slow as the stroke
of a lighthouse, the pull
of oars, pushing

a body's complex politics through time

and I want to drink mescal
again until everything's
familiar
patina burns
away, but I know
how much it costs, the after
-math, numberless
brain cells
drying over a dull ache,
the morning, slicing
like a sheet
of glass through damp
sleep . . .

One more
beer for the road
to Nogales
where there is pain
enough, and then some
joy, a trickle, a thin
rush at the sight of a woman's hands
piling shirts, hats, baskets,
the canvas above her head
so filled with sun
it looks like it could burst
into flame.

She steps through the doorway,
and curtain strings of obsidian beadwork
rearrange themselves like iron filings
in the force field of her slender figure.

She's late. Already the light
has begun to soften
the studio's white vehemence, the hard
shadows of January elms.

He sits at the drafting table.
Behind him the floor is a chaos
of discarded sketches
and black extension cords.
He nods but does not speak.
She moves to the stereo,
touches a power tab,
and invisible strings brighten the air
with a harpsichord sonata.

In the cleared space at the centre
of the room, she loosens
her shoulder straps
and lets the cream shift slide
into a wreath of shaded folds at her feet.

He watches her move, pliant
and lyrical, against the hardwood
floor's ruled page, and the tip
of his pen grazes the paper,
building a supple concordance
like strands of hair adrift in a stream.

He works through the night.
The blue star of his torch
bursts, again and again,
into a fountain of prickly sparks
until the obscure circuits,
the sinuous lines of force,
are fused, and flow
through nodes of dying fire.

Cooled on a walnut pedestal,
it looks as though the body's music,
the dancer and the dance,
have been stilled forever
in a complex cage of air,
but that fugue of intimate tensions
will revive and go on
through beautiful changes
if we should happen to walk around it
or turn it with our fingers in the sun.

Your body opens
a lexicon
of idioms: hands, hair,
the muscles around your knee,
thick ankles
and your hips, jigging
(Molly Bloom in a loose dress
on the bright, bare stage)
and when you leap
the sound
of your feet flat
on the wood
and the push
of your spread fingers
moves the air
in my lungs
like an undertow
and I
don't know
how but your eyes
when they look
up, at the end
release
my heart

SWEET TALK

DANCING IN THE MIRROR

for Annette

1

It's what you do to keep
your dream self apart
from critical paths, paper

clips, charts
and performance appraisals.
After work in the dark

you perform: *battement, arabesque, fouetté
en tournant* . . . to applause your heart
can rise from, though you know such things remain

theoretical. And while you dream, grown
-ups grow more the same
each day. Of course, the telephone

helps, but those few you could say
anything to, those you have known
for years, keep slipping away

into marriages, or solitudes of their own.
Alone: a relentless bell, crêpes
suzette and coffee, rooftop sunsets, stone

-ware and magazine photographs taped
to the fridge: rainbow decals: tricks
of light: house plants: albums: drapes:

then a weekend of concerts and casual sex.

2

Drunk shouts from the street melt
into sleep, and the dim, sleek
shapes cruise and cruise and strike
and you kick back through the bell
-buoy heart's red wash and break
out of breath, into dust,
into a clutter of old
clothes, old books. Slowly
you begin to trust
your ears: the ticking
snow, far-off echo-y
tires on wet streets, the sadness
of time. And there's no one to kiss
you to sleep again, so
you hug your pillow
hard to the hollow
undertow that aches and leaves
you weak, knees
to your chin,
your eyes pinched
against the corrosive light
that fades a sea-blue sky to white

3

ashes in the wind. You try to burrow
back under a spell
of soft inventions, but spurs

of punctual, actual day
have already started to press
in around your Japanese window shade.

Sparrows accelerate their helter-skelter
chatter and voices trapped inside
the wall seem to give off the practical smell

of coffee. From a snug wrap
of cottons and body-heat you slide
into the chill. Holding back

a bit, you spin
silent music out into trembling ferns
in warm rain at the edge of a lake, while thin

veils ignite and burn
the city behind you. Your skin
breathes and glows. You turn

everything off but the world
of blocked and reversed
light where the long rope of your hair, your curved

arms and smooth
legs race through a storm. Snowflakes
collect on the roof. Soon

you will have to choose
a disguise for the workplace.
One last kick and you come to rest, ease

your hair into a knot,
your thighs into loose denim.
Blouse. Knee socks. Hiking

boots. And your heart
adjusts to the throb
of stuck traffic. As you cross

the bridge, beautiful moves
inside your office outfit keep you
warm as those breakfasts of intimate silence

we share so rarely now,
and a thousand miles away I remember
how your grey-green eyes

dawned under cover of dusk in the park
that evening you teased
your kite from the shadows

of trees, higher
               and higher,
a wanderer tuned

by love to the changing sky.

Bach on the stereo. I'd like
to ride the rainbow shift
of a fugue, but this partnership
I have with silence drags
me back to the window: ice
-fog and hoarfrost:
styrofoam elms: the blue
beeps of a giant snow
machine. *Tools*
and bolts and steel drums
rust in the ghost towns
of the heart. Haunted by dreams
I never believed in myself,
I blame her soap opera cadenzas
on PMS and politics of the workplace,
but it doesn't help
and slowly the dismal overcast
revives a flaky movie of myself
as a kid, devouring lemon ice,
sucking the soiled, chlorinated
pleats of a paper cup,
and I'm back in my old neighbourhood
crushing the aftertaste in my fist,
letting it fall like a small
crime on the sidewalk
as Bach fades in the wind
that rattles the window
of the candy store on the corner
where unemployed layabouts
hang out most of the night
all summer long, punching
holes in their sweaty Ballantine Ales,
bitching about females, and spilling
four-part love songs into my sleep.

I thought we had learned
how to dissolve
self-importance into the sky
or the calm reach of a lake,
how to leave
some chaos in the shadows
of our lives. Why
stir up that pit
of reptile passion coiled
at the base of the brain?
Can it really matter
so much who
is at fault for the loss
of an address, the missed
appointment, the phone
call that should have been
returned, the broken
plate, the careless edge
of a phrase? When snow
collects in the apple tree
do we believe it will stay
forever? And when that frail
arrangement disintegrates
in a soft buffet of wind,
leaving so many branches
bare, do we try to change
or punish the air? You say
that letting things go
creates distance,
and distance is not love.
Not love, no, but the gap
love jumps to burn
at the heart of a storm.

1

Why do I still think of her voice
as an angel trapped in the soft rain of the shower?

I sit at the window, immobilized
by silence that jelled after she left
for work. The furnace clicks
and expires; air vents tick and the clock
in the kitchen whines like a stuck mosquito.

There are always risks. In love
even success can be stifling, like too much
ease. Soon we will drift
close again, get caught up and lost
as if in the pleasures of a magnetic storm,

but for now there is this tough stretch
of patience: winter outside, the apple tree
stranded in deep snow, its trunk mottled
like a thousand-year egg, its intimate crookedness
knotted against the glare of a stuccoed wall.

2

The wine's not ready to bottle yet.
It stands in the cellar, breathing
while earth draws the haze from its dubious past.

I can see myself in the highest branches, reaching
for half-rotten fruit,
tossing them into a plastic bucket

or shaking the tree so crabs will rain
down on the beautiful groundling
who gathers them up
and yells at me with her tangy voice
because I neglected to warn her
before I became a two-fisted storm
in the boughs, and suddenly
I'm surrounded by yellow-jackets.
They buzz my ears and tumble over my fingers,
nipping at brown pulp
and rising heavily into the air.

Once, when I was a boy,
they attacked and left me blind
for days, but now their bumpy flights
are openly disorganized
and it's clear that these childhood terrors
(helter-skelter war parties
gone astray in my hair
or stumbling over the nap of my flannel shirt)
have imbibed the spirits of wild yeast
and surprise themselves by melting
into fits of laughter I can't hear.

Let's go someplace
where the breeze is always
fresh and cool in the sun.

I'm reading your note, signed
love, on the patio at the club.
I turn in my chair
and the frame grates on the rain-pocked cement.

Above the burned-out lawn, grackles
veer and swoop like an obsolete air show.
A rude wind scatters papers
from this table-top *in the sun.*

Already the light has taken me
back to the streets of San Miguel,
where I stood, once, in the rinsed afternoon,
after thunder
-heads had melted and left the sky
pulsing with hypnotic heat waves
and a truck full of field hands knocked
me breathless, cheering
as I spun out into and over
the tables of a turista café,
and when I came to rest
on the flagstones, with the smell
of mesquite drying out
in my sinuses, a figure in black
pants and a white half-jacket asked
if there was something I desired.
Nothing, I said, thank you.
And as I lay there I noticed
how over the box-cut trees of the small jardín

the cathedral was beginning to soak
up the sunset
and when I could breathe
again, I wrote you a post-card, there
in my head, though years
would pass before a breeze from the sea
would scatter the shadows of your hair
over crossword puzzles,
and long-legged birds would come down from the sky
to walk on the sand, so awkwardly, their crooked feet
printing intricate codes where the waves turned
over and spread
their temporary mirrors *in the sun.*

> *Let's go someplace where the breeze comes up off the water,*
> *where the nights are soft and deep and full of stars.*
> *Let's walk through the empty streets of old stone cities,*
> *and out along a curved blade of sand, revived*
> *by the suddenly cold air and the sound*
> *of breakers toppling and hissing*
> *paving the beach with marble*
> *foam in the moonlight . . .*

Last week we sat and smoked in a thunderstorm
on the cedar deck behind our house, till we were
transported, by laughter and blue light and rain.

In the loose reef of lights across the bahía
only the beacon has a pulse, a small
flare that insists *I am here. You are there.*

Crickets are taking the night apart
with glassy ratchets, while carlights
like tiny pairs of eyes
flicker and close on the coast road.

Today I woke with the thought, *I have arrived
at the end of history.* I felt freed, even
from the strictures, vicissitudes
and consolations of a personal past.
I walked on a beach, lightened by that memory
loss. It seemed to go on, unbroken
until it disappeared beyond the horizon,
an endless avenue of damp sand, nearly white
where the sea erased all signs of passage,
and the sky was an infinite blue, utterly clear
of weather. A wonderful day, I thought,
a day without precedent or peer, but where
were you? Palm fronds riffed in the wind.
They sounded like a fresh deck of cards
shuffled again and again
by a player in no hurry to begin.
Then a flock of whistling sanates
came down to hop about the nearly invisible
tidepools, cocking their heads
as though they had just discovered
water. Their eyes glowed
– opals packed in soot –
and their long tails opened like fans
as they lay down their heads, their graphite beaks

working to scrape cool sips of sky
from the drying stone. When I looked again
through my Pentax they were gone.
I photographed bougainvillea: gaudy
petals without fragrance, fluttering
like dyed paper in the breeze . . .

                            It's past
midnight but I can feel the sun, burning,
driving out water and salt. The sea
explodes into the cliff below me. Smoke
hangs in the placid air. Back in the hills
a storm shimmers. And now, released
by the thick scruff of the forest,
green sparks drift and melt:
fireflies:
eccentric signals of hunger and sex.
Above them, a meteor scratches the dark
and evaporates, leaving no scar, no trace
of absence, even, on the night's bright face.

SYNERGY TRIAD

to Alison

for Lloyd

In this clear field, subjective weathers breed
only the ghost of a game plan. Intelligence, laughter,
and Beaujolais Nouveau before a good feed
loosen our time bonds. Your new lover, asking
and listening, my answers dissolving the need
for polite behaviour, your blue eyes flashing
with every exchange that reinvents the masculine
mystique, we bask in the absence of obsolete
codes and adjust a mix of lifelong momenta: [1]
world lines at matrix, this not-quite-random set
of selves rides the drift of leaderless energies
toward some unpredictable easement in the web
of human events, and it feels like we're directed
by an order that might exist beyond intervention.

Last night we drank wine. I
talked about music and you

listened. This afternoon, you
convinced me

to drive north, for the harbour,
the big sky and the sea.

Years ago, you wanted me
more than I

wanted you. Then you
left, and I wanted you

more than you wanted me.
Now, we

stand among hulls
and spars

close
but apart

watching the sun
pour through healthy clouds.

All through dinner, you
talk about painting and I

watch patterns rise
out of chaos. As the light dies

we walk on the sand
and look out over the water

where atmospheres
thrive in a timeless balance:

to the west, a furrow of soft fire,
to the east a night full of stars.

DOUBLE TALK

TWO VIEWS OF THE STREET

for Nick Tavuchis

On the corner, scuffling
dust, two little girls punch
a tetherball: bunched
papers in a plastic bag
tied with binder twine to the top
of a stop sign. Above the long street
with its beady, red-eyed tail-lights
and the yellow windows
of battered four-storey blocks,
elm twigs blacken. The sun
-set burns rose then magenta,
changing the pulse
of the city. Traffic thins
and a few cars push
through the briefly magical afterlight
with a sound like forced air
and the spritz of tires over
leftover sand.

A husky mood
near silence turns
into night, and it comes
again, the whole
past, absentminded love, a child
at an open window looking down
out of loneliness
into the street, into his life

to come, which is already more
than half gone
and a thousand miles away
it's me, looking out
through another cold spring
evening, thinking of home,
wondering what it was
and how it has kept
such distant memories wet
with feeling, like a set
of slides, in a box
in the small back room
off the kitchen, all these years.

Time rests here. The click
of plastic (blue chip
red chip) pitched at intervals
under a solo bulb onto green baize
is the risky signature that opens,
behind these measured smiles,
a mute fantasia, episodes
of hope, cadenzas of clenched elation
drained by sudden turns
of luck.
         And though we conduct
ourselves harmoniously, we
are diminished, now
that the off-beat jokes, ritual scores
of ball games, and the slick
runs of macho repartee
have been resolved –
with round after round
of major calculations, minor drinks –
into the tension of a stoned quintet
who sit slumped in blue haze, retarded,
syncopated, but still
tuned in, our faces fixed
in some Dorian mode like a painting: *Men
at Play*, while grey
ash drops exhausted scales
onto wrist hair and shirtfronts and sharp lapels.

A glass throws its belled shadow
across the felt
like a charcoal scherzo. It's
one of those helium balloons
ready to sail but moored

to the next Scotch, the next
card. Sustained, steady
under the improvised grunts, the creak
of a chair, the hoarse
glissades of overlapping breath
(slurs, whistles
through sinuses tuned by years
of cigarette smoke, factory smoke,
smoke of an old war) I can hear it:

the flat static
of a radio that ran out of songs
when the bars closed
and a last late voice broke for the night.

Why do your stories
glamourize life?

I suppose because life
sucks and I can't
escape from my species,
our toys of death,
our talk about the world
economy. I hear
blood at the edge
of extinction. Even
champagne brings me down.

Do you write
for the People?

Undifferentiated motor
skills? No. I write
to keep our minds away
from the latest weapons.

A closet reformer
dispensing sugar-coated
fantasy pills?

Yes.

What for?

It brings in money which I take
to the pub. It keeps
dreamers home nights.
It's cheaper than cocaine.

Maybe it even curbs the body
count . . .

But what about
the history of ideas?

Ideas don't have
histories, they just go
out of style. History
itself is a bad idea.

You mean thinking about
the past is a waste of time?

I mean the past is not
history, which is only
what we think we know
about what might have happened.

But there are
records, documents . . .

Cave paintings,
dinosaur footprints, old
magazines, and stuff
like that? Sure.
And all the shapes we take
before we're born. Trouble
is we think it works
like a toaster. Daylight
is cosmic nuance, Jack. Blood
spurting and smoking won't
change a goddam thing.

In one sentence, how
would you like us to think of your work?

In two words, don't
bother.

- *Black*

Woolly-minded nabobs
hoard the junktime
dancers jive
away. Long ago, they
took up slaving
for a living, loving
ethnic restaurants and shortfall gold.

They squaffed buzzwords
and flag flap, impressed
by decadence, by body
counts that match the national debt.

What's that you say, the market
fell on its ass? Look, dark
is when the lights come on.
All good sheep know that.

- *White*

Clouds. Fuzzy
water high on the blue
planet: little puffs
of stuff, suds, popcorn
faces and soft
animals. Why not
admit it, laziness
is closer to god
and cleaner too
than work. Afternoons

of angel hair. Rums
and coke. But sometimes
bliss comes inside out
like a glove, the jazz
of hyper achievers proves
contagious, and midnight
oil corrupts our aimless mornings.

(selected, arranged, and re-written
from one of John Newlove's notebooks)

1

The Kootenays, valley
of lost causes. A grey
afternoon.

I'm reading a book about forebears.

> *These, she exclaimed,*
> *are only my gardening pearls.*

What did I trade
for this non-profit life?

2

Non enim pro angelis mortuus est Christus.

True. But can I be sure he died for me?
Or, to put the question differently,
how may a man reveal his absolute nature?

Mark this day with a white stone.

3

It's not the end of the physical world
but the end of our dream

of the world that keeps me awake
nights, also

flesh doesn't heal from the core
as quickly or completely
as it did before,

and words can still defeat me,
fact or metaphor
reaching too deeply

till even the bones are sore,
reacting, meekly,
grating at the door

of sleep. A nightly
absence more and more
invites me,

more and more
the dark re-writes me:
hollow at the core.

4

What will death be like?
Will the sky
slam
shut
on a ship-shape grave?

One tries not to act
in accordance with one's darkest beliefs,
though they appear
irrefutable.

5

In Flores, Guatemala,
there are more cormorants than people.

6

A self-possessed whisky baritone
silences the smoke-filled room:
the real meaning of life . . .

I've been reading a book about forebears:

> *Typical of many was the Welsh gentleman who changed his
> coat of arms at The Conquest from three bloody Saxon heads to
> three closed helmets.*

7

The violence of idleness
invades me.

I read another, longer book:

> *No matter how clever he is, or how skilled in argument, a man
> who has willingly fettered his intelligence should not be listened
> to with any respect when he presumes to speak on intellectual
> matters. Adherence to any doctrine whatever is such a fettering.
> He may be listened to only when he speaks of his own province
> factually, and then with suspicion.*

The question to ask the universe is not
why am I here, but why
should this exist around me?

8

Who lies here lived
desired by she
who laments his untimely departure

Could anyone rest easy
under such a heartfelt epitaph?

9

You must know when to panic
and when to smile like a stone.

10

She said, with a shrill
but stagey horror, holding
one hand to her throat:
"There's a *gentleman*
in a *green suit* to see you."

The Lord Elgin Hotel, 9 a.m.
A loud voice: "They only have
Cream of Wheat!"

Earth is a very noisy planet.

11

If we're alone
in the universe
we're freaks

but don't let that
depress you, think
of it this way:

our destiny
has always been to test
the threshold of pure intelligence.

12

By the time I learn how to smile
there is nothing to smile about.

Industrial nations crumble
and latecomers rise
like a tainted breeze
from the ruins of exploitation.

What more
is there to do
or say? Let time have its way
while we offer appropriate gestures
of condolence.

*One does not need
to cut a man's throat
once one has poisoned his soup.*

13

There are such crowds now
in the rent-free chambers of death
we can all afford to feel
briefly immortal.

CATCH

In the narrow
passage between
islands where the rip tide
turns, they
let their boats
drift, slipping
the craft of millennia
into that now
alien
atmosphere, the sea.

Living
silver
tumbles
into the dark
hold as neurons
fire – a gap
in the breath,
a skipped
pulse
at slithery harvest.

So much death
and life at once
makes the head spin
like the double talk
of oracles, or the sting
and flutter of Greek
songs, at night, in the tavernas
where something fresh
out of time comes back
to dance inside them.

POACHED GRILSE

What is the law, out here, where there's no other
boat in sight? We take what we need from the sea
as we've always done, each of us, privately,
and if they won't rise to the bucktail's yellow feather
dancing from sixty yards of line, smothered
in foam, in the sun, for hours, then I'll go deep
with a spinner strung from illicit weights, creeping
through chuck, trolling two slack jigs for cover.

Hauling them in on the wire, half asleep
from the cold, I can see them as rainbows, firm & clean
with the hard shimmer of silver and polished stone.
But there's no sport in this. Chilled to the bone,
I take one more for an old friend who has flown
thousands of miles with a crisp white from the Rhone.

BACK TALK

DON'T GO AWAY

a strong tanned hand grips the pool railing in opulent sunlight

pretty feet in sandals approach and pass

long feminine legs lounging and crossing in unison

then the frosty bottle of Labatt's Light

behind it but only partly obscured
a girl in a floppy hat
opens her hot
pink
lipstick
smile

what next? wholesome
bodies in brief
clothes
looking as though they've just
sprung
back intact from a quick
toss on the sheets

and after that this adolescent
polar bear, bewildered, half out of
the ice, transformed by industrial photography
into a frosty pilsner beer glass,
foam right to the rim,
and behind that the satisfied smirk

of a man whose mouth remains
closed, his eyes
obscured by a big straw hat

so

does a Labatt's Light
keep you sexy and young,
let you conquer the wilderness,
get you love, get you money

are white bears just out of puberty
stupid because they don't know how to make it
(or steal it or persuade
with their considerable powers
of persuasion others to make it for them)

and

do both human sexes find happiness
when they are allowed to display
up-to-date swimsuits in expensive surroundings
which they can afford
because they have learned to resist
Dom Perignon and Rémy Martin

or what?

don't answer that
until you've poured yourself a double

by then
your favourite private eye
will be back breaking
the case of the missing
brain stem

and stand-in stunt men
will serve up the usual chaser

after this important message

He's drinking a Heineken, straight
from the bottle, waiting
for a plane.
           Across the bar
a snubnosed youth machine smiles
an imperial smile over her caesar.
All she wants is to fill for a while
the wrinkled organ asleep inside
his pants.
           He stares back. He can't
help imagining how his tongue, already
chemically dead from too many Rothman's,
would taste if it gently insinuated
the tip of itself into the salty scratch
and slide of her pubes, and his eyes flicker
a bit, but his cock continues to
hibernate like a stuffed pundit.

She senses and resents its indifference,
irate because how dare this burned-out
slime ball in a JC Penney suit
undress her with his eyes and sip
his beer and blow fat smoke rings at her
invincible glamour. She can almost feel
his democratic imagination freely
anointing the tight halo between her tanned
buttocks, then slipping its tongue, inch
by ounce, through the glistening lips
of her cunt. She squirms on the barstool,
snaps her attention away, but when she looks
back she is thrilled by his eyes

which see her now in morning light,
naked after a shower,
drawing white cotton over her thighs
and snugging it into her crotch,
and as he starts to caress
the curve of her ass and the long trough
of back muscle in which her spine
lines up like a caravan of baldheaded monks,

she hears this male voice, laughing
in its throat, saying please, I'll buy you
a microwave, a Porsche, an island off the coast
of Venezuela, a tin banana executed by the hottest
sculptor in Ecuador, if only you'll agree to sit
still while I pump a spurt or two of hot wet
feathers into the only grip you'll ever have
on supply-side economics. It's for your own
good, believe me, you'll think
it's nifty, you have no idea
how it can improve
the taste of clamato and vodka, and now

she's really seeing red, she tosses
her hair, crushes her cigarette
out and her eyes recharge, but he won't

stop, he's into it, and there
she is again, in a soft-focus meadow, wearing a blue
straw hat, white gloved hand dreamily fingering
that taut nub of tissue under a flowered skirt,
her wrist moving delicately, bumping against the purple clover
blossoms that have already begun to fall
asleep on their short stems, and suddenly he is
overwhelmed by a brutish need to love her forever
as the disembodied voice that likes to keep

these chance encounters from getting out of control
announces his flight, and he stands and heads
without a backward glance, toward the 747
whose thrust will push him up and into and through
immaculate folds that soften the sky.

When our eyes, though we can feel them sag after a long hard day at the farm, or the conference of experts on a particular aspect, or a simple week at the pub shooting pool and contemplating, sporadically, the joys and glooms of intermittent employment, after these long hard times which we all understand, why, when our eyes meet the eyes of a stranger, do we begin to smell the incense of salvation?

Hmmn, that's an odd question. But it worries me. I'm old enough now to have been entirely let down by these moments of subtle heart-race and glandular assurance. Once we begin, though, to banter and flirt, once we begin to believe it is crucial to share our inconclusions, our media dreams, our belief in clothes and mirrors and mild shampoos, then, well, a swift shadow crosses the light . . .

So. French onion soup, candles, and later a bottle of vintage port with Havana cigars from before the revolution. We drive each other crazy and we're glad, though we continue to scour the world for eyes of topaz, eyes of jade: impossible saviours dressed in impeccably tailored cloth, stepping elegantly out of the ads, out of the finest magazines, the most expensive posters, retaining that fragile, that instantly recognizable gloss of perfection, which begins, alas, to deteriorate, even before we can exchange a few empty words. Nevertheless, we have come together in this flashy historical moment, drawn by a mutual desire to escape the commonplace and rise to a higher standard of decay.

The televised ads
for divinity have changed
coin from idol work
-manship into realm
insignia. This confirms
His place in the kingdom
of things, because, well,
the only visible difference
between those who are saved
and those damned
few who have broken
with the *Zeitgelt* lies
in their god-given ability
to consume. Glass
temples high and bright
as the skylines of commerce
have already done much to expand
the needle's eye. Consider this
eloquent barker bespeaking The Lord:
his cloth-of-gold suit,
his five year media contract,
and of course that coached
voice tugging at all
the strings implanted
painlessly as we sauntered
in our spare time through malls and centres,
filling our minds with acres
of junk. *Believe,* he whispers
believe in the one with the most
expensive haircut.

Those who sing so arrestingly
about the lonely night are actual
-ly, at this time, asleep
in their expensive beds
while we dream they are singing
for us, that they know
what keeps us awake and away
from our lives which are not
what they should be. Forty-Eight
bars and the prison
of failed love dissolves
in the small hours
where ice ticks
like a stuck valve in the heart
of a streetlight
and the elms are dressed
exactly like that last
goodbye. But when the record
stops there is no comfort,
there is only the sadness of time
that has no voice, apart
from the wind, which does not sleep
even in the expensive beds
of flowers in the park
where we walk sometimes
on nights like these, talking
to ourselves as light comes up
into the tall grey clouds.

IMMANENT DOMAIN

to john moriarty in ireland

      for brian, margaret, victor, gerry, valdine,
      arthur, lucy and david

Slides of mystical vistas
dissolve the dining-room wall
as your voice comes to us
through the banal miracle of a cassette
speaking of journeys and searches and quests
and I want to tell you I have discovered
that quest is commitment to stasis,
that searches fail
to let the *tao* flower and be,
that journeys only teach us to love
the road that goes back
to what we never leave and cannot remember,

but how can I say, after all these years,
what it's like when the mind explodes
everything you think of as your life,
the ice I wanted for company then
as most of us want fire,
the years coming of age
inhaling the incense of Sunlight detergent,
looking out at the worst part of the city,
the snow coming down
through streetlights and bare branches
with that hissing sound
I learned to care for with my empty heart,
the big white Lincolns and midnight blue

Le Barons that miss the turn below my window,
thump into the trunk of an elm,
and back off with clinking radiator fans?

I hear your voice, complex
as water over stone,
and I want to explain

that the mysteries you speak of
reside in basement laundry rooms,
in the charcoal
a six-foot-four and happily lonely
neighbour lights after work,
his battered car door open,
his aluminum beer cans frosting
beside the hibachi,
burgers and bread smoking
like a sacrifice in the summer air,
in the obese woman
I found wandering among the garbage cans
long after midnight,
barefoot in a satin slip,
babbling some twisted story
about blankets and cigarettes,
her breath a miasma
of alcohol and sugarless gum,

that I am no longer persuaded
by searches and journeys and quests

that the lord of unspeakable horror and joy
is the street at night after rain
where I lean my overheated consciousness
out of a speeding car
and watch the numberless half-erased faces

of pebbles gleaming and slipping away
like lives that serve and wear out
gladly on better days,
bitterly and with indignant gloom
on days when I refuse to get off my ass
and sing, if only to myself,
quietly screwing
braces into a crooked wall
that will hold white shelves
of terrycloth and cotton
in the newest shabby apartment
the beautiful sister of a friend
has taken on a temporary basis
while she drinks and works
at loving an unhappy man
who has wasted his life
on journeys and searches and quests,
who may stumble over a dozing animal
one night on his way
home from the pub and feel its cry
melt in his blood, opening
his clenched heart like a rose.

• *Offing a State Bird*

A shrill mote
silenced
by exhaust pipes
settles on the Bell
Telephone wire
and fills the Weaver Scope
's blue manhole: folded
yellow-gold
wings with black (soot
from the ducts
of commerce?) tips
in which the split
crossed
hair of precision
dissolves (the news report
will be controversial,
cameras will bleed
machine oil and gunpowder smoke
through a complex of lens rings)

"Squeeze, don't pull."

A cr   ack accelerates
down country roads

The tail ex p l   O   D   E   S
The headpiece-and-bodice
                       r
                       o
                       p
                       s

Down hangs in the air like soul stuffing

• *Speaking Out*

Half drunk but sharp as a tack
Ist eerm yse lftot hepodium

The hillside is packed
with eyes ideas posters rhetorical stands
and bands whose decibels burst
brains like balloons
under the stars   Delirium
swims over the trees
like bits of light over a prom
gymnasium's window dressing

I clear my throat

"Our aim now
must be to squeeze off a shot
at the city's nest of uniforms,
credential photos,
and media hindsights"

Applause
like developing newsprint

All summer long
the parks fill with police and mosquitos

1

We have overcome.
There's no doubt about it.
Just look at our ingenious modes
of peregrination: vehicles
driven by contained fossil-fire, high
-ways gracefully rib
-boning the dust
-free hills and vales, and see
how we've planted beside them
at calculated intervals
towering rustfree ironstemmed seedlings
whose pods ignite
with a diamond or topaz glow
automatically as darkness
threatens, disempowering
the irresponsible action of clouds,
the impractical slivers, blades, flood
-lights and black moods of the moon.

2

At the College
Pub, under ferns
whose lineage pre-dates
the dinosaur, a Professor
flutters his wrinkled eyelids
and sighs among protegés, raises
the weathered skin of a stiff neck
against the self-serving mythologies
of media politics and the popular mind

then turns toward the multilayered floor to
ceiling glass that affords a disinterested view
of the footpaths and avenues dappled by cathedral elms
whose leaves have been chewed to a fine lace once again
by small   green   worms.

SEPTEMBRR

it's the season of smoke,
pencil sharpeners, boredom.

leaves
released leaves
leaves that have been let
go go oh
only so far

    (should I say
    like us?)

but it's all quite
entertaining, don't you agree? the
schoolkids in their new clothes
brisk flurries whisking and scraping
over pavements in the crisp air . . .

till the trees run out of encores
and we remember
silver. then
the wind bites without hunger.
the clocks repeat
themselves, time out of mind.

rock is not the bottom.
there is no bottom.
there are no lines either.

there is money, of course,
but never enough.

there is moonlight and water.
there is romance. there are children.
and acrobats. and those who kill for fun.

there are lists and promises.
there are betrayals. dust

comes in through tight windows.

there are dreams
that make us
crazy and sad
when we suck them
from TV screens
all the way into our blood.

there are birds, graceful
silhouettes in just the lightest
wash of blush magenta near the end
of day. and there are birds
who eat the young of other birds.

there is the sea
endlessly rocking

stones
at the edge
of the mind. and there

are tiny survivors
the eye can't see
who split and go on
splitting, and the first
is also the last
because they're one
and the same.

STATEN ISLAND FERRY

July 4, Nineteen Eighty Something

for R. H.

A day like this
comes loose from its year tag.
Whitman would understand.
Or maybe not. It was just
so windy, and The Statue
of Liberty suffered
as though for the first time
in her life the indignities
of American know-how: scaffolding
from knee to crown
and all the way up the arm that bears
the torch. There were workers
ant-like at their trades
in the smoky sunset. There were gulls
squawking and fighting, picking
tidbits out of the garbage
that boiled in the wake of the fat
slow boat. There were travellers
crowding the rails
with cameras and zoom lenses,
trying to freeze this moment
into their lives. And in spite of the wind
it was hot. The air was heavy.
The bodies of the passengers
were heavy. But I raised
my Pentax and it all
made sense: the sweating African face
under a cotton headdress, his eyes
gold in the waning sun, and beyond

the sleek curve of his cheek, The Lady
of Easy Ideas, drenched
in flame and shadow, more
unapproachable than ever
behind the struts and platforms
of her long overdue
reconstruction. Then someone
jostled my arm and the shutter
snapped, captured
a blurred wing, a faint
star on the soiled horizon.

Twenty below and they're bundled in blue
parkas. They look like makeshift astronauts
on the moonscape roof of the Legislature
more than a hundred feet above Earth.

One of them dips a stick with a tin can
screwed to its end into a smoking drum on wheels
and lifts it, nailholes leaking a thick black rain
that fills a scraped square with glossy threads

like a Pollock painting, forward and
back in a cobra dance while his partner shakes
crushed tyndalstone from the ringing blade
of a shovel, then there's a break in the rhythm.

The tar spreader backs his drum two giant steps
dreaming of rum, maybe, or a game of eight ball
as a bearded man who looks like he just stepped out
of a Budweiser ad arrives with a red wheelbarrow

from the edge where pulleys and ropes flex in the wind
and restores the mound of gravel. Down
on the ground a man with a Sherlock Holmes pipe cranks
a handle and the tipped tub spills gleaming

asphalt into a dented bucket. A cake of white
smoke slides off and shreds like fog in the wind.
Creaking wheels and cables drag it up, and up
to another parka with frosted eyebrows

who lifts the wire handle in one thick fist, spits
a still-smouldering roll-your-own like a cherry pit right

over the edge and hauls the already thickening ooze
(the bucket's cracked black skin flickering in the vodka

light) to the nearly empty drum. In one
quick move he lifts and pours blue smoke, then
essence of pine and ancient fern, sleek
as a crow's wing, drowning the can on a stick

which the spreader levers up again and sweeps back
and forth, trailing its curtain of hot licorice,
and the man with the oversized shovel sprays a controlled
patter of gravel, and waits, while the cables dance

at the edge of the roof and above the horizon
the light goes beige as tyndalstone. With the first
rumours of night a bruise collects along the underside
of a cloud and the rhythm breaks, and the rhythm starts

again, and soon the roof is good for another term
and they all stand loose for a while, watching
the sky boil up and advance, a storm front
whose dark veins begin to discolour what's left of the sun.

when the reporter asked him why
he was in Honduras, "We can't
have communists running
around loose, doing
whatever they want." He was a freedom
enthusiast with a gun. Dumbocracy
surged in his face: youthful
and oddly beautiful in the light
of the ordinary canefield whose leaves
knew nothing except how to grow. What
clarity of feeling, I thought, how
can you criticize such courageous
obedience? Well, it gags
reality, this mouth without a thought
in its head that hasn't been put there,
this fiercely moral
boy scout with a full
clip and a cause, this great
white hope.

       When I was a kid long ago
I heard it on the radio: the Lone
Ranger's handmade bullets whanged
and whizzed, unerringly disarming
the bad guys who were always just
a split second slower because
they were the bad guys. I even read
the book in which he got shot
and Tonto nursed him back from the edge
of terrible inactivity, in a house of pine
boughs deep in the woods. But even after
such an ordeal he would never
shoot anyone in the head or the crotch

or give a darn how silver fared
on the stock exchange. Independently
wealthy, he could afford to let
the banged up softnoses lie
where they fell, all over the West.
Always, he knew how to right
what was wrong and always he sang, Heigh
Ho Silver, Away. I thought about his horse
a lot, a metal slickness dissolving light
from the muscles and tendons, his mane
a flurry of angel hair, his hooves, bright
battering sandals (Hopkins), his nostrils
pink, his breath nearly capable
of discourse.

           I wonder
now if this young Newsweek
hero-to-be in his fresh
fatigues would be interested
in the words that made me believe
the Ranger alone on the wide frontier
with his grunting sidekick Tonto
could never be mistaken or unfair
and that he roamed at one actual time
in the past and might have talked
(briefly, of course, in his usual
laconic manner which is not,
alas, my own) with Abraham
Lincoln, or Teddy, or one
of the other Capitalized
leaders of the pack. Once you begin
to imagine the bullet's path
and all that might happen
around it, the technology seems
like a miracle. *Inhuman.*
Of the veritable Ocean (Stevens)

of dreamstuff and so
this morally conditioned upright
Son of Sam (the uncle) wants to shoot
his way to the heart of the problem.

    A little town in Texas,
    the last movie show,
    black and white, and the wind
    sadder and older and emptier even
    than static or dead air
    on that Atwater-Kent
    my grandparents closed
    their bouncy conversations
    down for, listening
    to Roosevelt's funeral
    as though it would actually pass
    through the living room
    while the sun held fire
    in the paper shade all afternoon . . .

Soldier, I salute
your priceless
commitment. Don't
come home. Get
your hand
-les on the situation, force
the red menace to think
twice before it fucks
with a cloned ranger (charged
as he is with the flap
of stars and striplings).

    Interlude: Tonto, your loyalty
    was never a question, the shit
    work you did without resentment
    serving the star of the show.

Dignified servility. What a team
you were. Historic antagonists
working to save the world
from bandits and bullies and asshole
views. Never mind that your kin
exploded
with alcohol, smallpox, and other
improvements. Forget the politics
of genocide, justice
in the land of the free demands
this tiny concession because,
without you, the masked saviour
of banks and ranches and farms
will suck air and sift
off into the dry canyons
merely the ghost of a good idea
who can only make white history
wash too late. So.

Don't go near the border, boy.
Hold off on Nicaragua.
In the meantime, you can play
with your impressive toys
and fill your canteen with boiled agua.
Next time the camera pokes a cyclops eye
into your life, be ready to improvise,
if only on the junk you learned in school.

These tireless purveyors of belief
dress conservatively and hijack the sky machines
of godless knowledge. They know they are here for a brief
time only, so they are brave, and their keen
sense of show biz never wavers. They promise
to shoot the unclean souls out of kids and ladies
every hour on the hour unless
their demands for prime-time coverage, maid
service, the lifting of naval blockades, a tank
-ful of godless knowledge, hot dogs, lemonade,
and an honorarium from The World Bank
are seen to without delay. A Commando *RAID!*
kills them dead. (Also some ladies and kids).
The TV byte pans to the pyramids.

darkness blacker than soot even.
is this the night? the abyss?
it's what you saw, bleeding
in the tub, and did not want
to enter. *rage fades
into loneliness and fear.* what
did you learn? not to trade
your conscience for a pocket
of silence compressed under megatons
of Egyptian stone? wrists leak
a royal decor into tepid water.
*i wait for death to ferry me across
the rest of a life i couldn't solve
when i ran it through in my head.
it was the dark that drove me
back, to my feet, dripping wet,
scattering blood on the tiles,
the sill, the clean shag rug.*

the cops came. they poked you
with nightsticks. they used
their felony voices to change
your already broken idea
of yourself into cowardice
as you sat there handcuffed,
wrapped with an old sheet
in the back of their Ford.

why did you start to enjoy
this new career as a traitor?
piece of shit, they said.
should have stayed in the tub.

at the station, the day
officer mouthed words
as he typed . . . *crime*
against the people . . . attempted.
they made you wait with the others.
you sat on a wooden bench
for seventeen minutes before
you got up and left. they
called you at home. you can't
do that, they explained. do what?
leave after being booked and without
the proper clothing. however
we've talked it over
with your wife, your employer,
and because no one was willing
to press charges, you're free
to go. but i already
went, you said. yes, we
can corroborate that information,
but please be advised, it will remain
on your sheet as a matter of record.

correct. and that was when
i first understood. it.
i never wanted to die.
i wanted to prove that i could
act
        crazy, like everyone else.

Trains rust on the tracks.
For years, the parks
have been closed to civilians. Books
may be accessed
at airports and bus stations only.

Once, we believed it was possible
to understand what went on
around us: Dawn. Rain
in the streets. Then
shop became a verb: the universe
opened and wouldn't stop rushing
away. We discovered that God
was money and vice
versa. Now we're obsessed
by clothing. If a child
runs naked into the street
it will be taken by agencies,
given new fingerprints,
and raised by humanoids on the moon.

Persiflage
sells more albums
than all other bands combined.

There is one newspaper
published locally
under thousands of different names.

Even casual sleep
is monitored by satellite.
Those who forget their dreams

can buy them back
on video for a nominal fee.

Last year the birds left early.
Now the sky is clear
as a bell jar. Leaves
turn black and blue but never
fall. Snowflakes
burn unrepeatable designs
into our hands and faces.
Puddles glow in the dark.

South of Toronto
a forty-foot yawl
leaves a lime-green ghost on the lake
as it fades (for a fee)
into some less stressful dimension.

We're crazy for gasoline.
Those who can still afford it
dab it under their arms and behind their ears
spray it into their genital hair
pat it onto their faces after a shave.

The future trembles like a mirage
in a bowl full of colourless jello.
Those who have bought it
polish their silver spoons.

TALKING TO MYSELF

HORIZONS

The overcast breaks up and sunlight
spills into the street. I'm driving
across town toward the river. *Between*
backlit tenements, a flare of gold,
a promise, breathless as Romance,
burns, chaotic but pure, beyond the last
wrought iron fence. Well, it's just
the mind of the child surfacing
for a while before the day retreats
into smoke, and the parkway leads me home.

Exquisite how when the highway lights
come on the sky backs off. Cashmere
collar, calfskin gloves, the smell
of a new car, fingernails trimmed
and growing, everything I dreamed
I could be I've become and its eerie
aura surrounds me. I've travelled. I remember
sunlight tumbling through clouds over broken columns,
retsina in copper cups and sparks
rising from open fires in the agora at night.

Once, in Rome, I watched a Tintoretto
sky collect above the Piazza di Spagna.
The fountain gathered overtones
of dusk into gorgeous foam. My life
completed itself and I was afraid.
What could I hope for
if my heart could melt

so easily into the leap
and crash of water? Light
drained from the air and I moved on.

How the great writers understood
the self-sufficiency of moments like those.
And yet they had to go on with their stories.
Anna Karenina dives under a train. The Roman
Consul bleeds in a stone tub. The hunchback
buries himself alive with the corpse
of Esmeralda. I want to drive all night.
I want to be ragged, unshaven, hungry, and lost
in the dawn. I want to believe
that something will happen to change me.

In the empty
Safeway
parking lot
after a stormy night

      in a black
      depression
      filled with rain

water, oil
refines the drab light
to a garish rainbow –
chartreuse, magenta, peacock blue –

      then the painful
      fiesta of dawn
      begins

and suddenly it's clear
that I am a part of the morning,
the part that watches
while it burns.

calendar song

ice cracks in the glass. a universe
of molecules rearranges itself: water,
carbon dioxide, vodka, lime juice, and particles
of dust from the breeze that comes in
through the window, softly
prescribing autumn, a turning
at which it is appropriate (though perhaps absurd)
to make resolutions:
                              don't drink too much, but give
your arteries a daily sluice. work
the large muscle groups, especially the heart,
but only to the slightest burn.
don't persist or persevere.
just do what needs to be done. avoid
christmas like the plague. drive out
under the sky and sit there
quietly among the ticks and fumes
of the cooling motor, thinking
of nothing, letting your husk
of selves dissolve in the effortless night.

go home and sit down by the fireside's light.
convince your self-image to jump in the river
and put a stop to this thing you have about final manoeuvres.

Board a winter afternoon
bus from Winnipeg
to Brandon. Soon the narcotic ice
light will transport you
to a space buggy, droning
across the face of an abandoned
planet, no one
on the roads, the glare
of sundogs like matched
trumpet notes, the fields overcome
by low dunes, white
and sleek as quicklime, smoking
where the continuous gale
whets their curved
lips and the delicate beige
bones of weeds flutter
from terraced wind-prints,
and now, out of nowhere,
out of a desolation so
pure it's aesthetic, this
graveyard without a fence
like an extinct colony
of stones – weathered
inscriptions half silted up
with alkali snow, shadows
inching toward a locked
horizon – passes

      under glass in the sun
      as if those yesterdays
      had closed like an air
      tight case in a museum

when did I first become aware
that I would un-
become sometime in the future?
some time in the past. now,

in the future I feared
then, I'm afraid
I won't achieve
that unbecoming late

enough. buying insurance
before the double rums on routine
flights, waking bewildered
by dreams of a black

faint, I know, I can feel
it surround me, the bristle
of Harris Tweed, the blast
of thirty-below

air that takes my breath
away. I pay
my parking tickets
early. I answer

letters the day they arrive.
I think of the future without
me in it, I make out my will:
do this, do that,

organize my aftermath
in an orderly fashion. I feel
better, I stop at a bar,
order a Diet Pepsi and watch

college basketball on the tube.
one of the heavy
dunkers with a pro
career in his future crumples.

I know he won't come back.
how do I know? I watch
my diet. I walk up the six
flights to my office. I swallow

vitamins with skim milk each morn.
I lose weight. I quit
smoking. I take
vacations once or twice

a week. sometimes, I look
at my hands, how puffy, how
wrinkled they have become.
I put off sex for a day

or two, and it all comes back,
the excitement, the rise
and rise and failed
muscle tone at the end,

and she says how good
you are to wait, to defer
what must be irresistible just
because you care. I go

about my business. day
by week by month, without the slightest
rupture in my performance. but later, after
the silence returns, there is this

privacy. tomorrow I will buy
a peg for the bridge of my guitar.
I will play it again. this time
for no one at all. and I will sing

the old songs, the rhymes
coming due, as the chords
change, and I will hear thin dimes
fall against each other on the boards

of a juke joint in Mississippi
where once in the dream time
of my youth I slipped free
from the numbness, the grime,

the stench of the factory, the machine
's thump and slather, into this
fingering, this lean
tight voice and the bliss

of twelve-bar blues, over
and over and over again.
Green Corn. Dust My Broom. Clover
Hitch and Old Black Betty. When

I finish and put up my Martin, I have this
long night ahead of me, in which I can sleep,
in which I can putter, get pissed,
or try to come to terms with the deep

and slow exhaustion of my system. The cells
themselves give up a little every day. And the song
comes without effort, now, if I want it, like the bells
of a church in a town no one lives in any more, a strong

sound out of time, Old Mexico, where nothing went wrong
for a while until the magic of money came south over the hills
invisibly, and everyone began to notice their options. Bong.
Bong. And so on. I can rhyme it. I can feel it. Chills

ripple over me. Of course they are symbolic. Archetypal too.
It's late. My joints creak, even though I haven't moved
my ass for an hour. Everything, even the night, is blue
these days. Dig it. Take it in. What does it prove?

This. Little signals, little indications. They began
almost when I did. Letdowns after lunch. Dreams
in which the colour is not as vivid as it used to be, and
a sense that, whatever you do, whatever intricate schemes

you can actualize, you'll somehow end up soiled by chagrin
or driven awry by envy and ambition. How do I get by
the attitude that won't allow me to die
without a deep sense of failure, angst, bad karma, and sin?

Learn to lie down in the desert of bones and rocks.
Learn to accept the inevitability of unmatched socks
every time you open the door of that voracious dryer.
Work at what hours you please. Try to get higher

on things like answering letters, paying bills, going out
in the late light for a walk, touching the leaves, knowing
that no one is there, though your life is rich with friends
and lovers, rivals and critics, and all those valuable others.

no one is there to help re-invent the immense possibilities
you really believed lay before you, before, in your youth.
in everyone's youth. *do what you love to do, the money will come
later.* hit men nod, wisely, playing chess, making their wills

before a painless death in a Texas prison. they don't mind,
really, lying back on a hospital gurney – narrow bed on wheels
to speed their after stuff to the oven – they are clear.
why did you do it? I don't know, it wasn't much

to write home about, there was just this rush. I know
what he means. we've all had the impulse. remember that cartoon
The Urge to Kill? i've murdered multitudes in my head.
enjoyed it too, but in the flesh i'm not ready

to swat even one mosquito, never mind the shit-for-brain cops
who catch me out on the streets late, and act out their script
about keeping everything safe, by force, naturally, but how
can they get off, in the small hours, on the luxury of bop

-ping a slightly eccentric citizen with their sticks
then dropping him off at the detention centre? when the she
-male pulled her .357 i laughed, but she stuck it in my ribs.
blonde, she was. serious and committed. we should all be

committed, the way we behave these days. i've done it
myself. no surprise there. how can the soul thrive
on choco-milk? or gatorade? or squirt? or even the more
effective liquids we sip to get happy. too late for that.

i might never be happy. so what. i'm tired of chasing
it. when the butterfly of delight lands on my fist
i'll probably suck it into my mouth and chew it and swallow
it and wait through that seasick drop for the two-hour high.

or else I'll remember what happens after happiness and take a deep
breath and blow it back into its difficult and unprofitable life.
we dream we could have been much more . . . could have shone
better than anyone else with the same credentials.

Twinkle, twinkle, little star.
Only astronomers wonder where you are.
And they only wonder because if they wonder enough
and collect verified data, they can get grants.

believe me it's not easy this dredging for images this cadence
hopping always trying to invite the bottoms of wells to tea always
tired always a little disappointed even after a particularly good
phrase because you know it will be followed by a not particularly
good phrase and what's it all for anyway since only a few friends
and competitors will bother to read what you labour over and they
will be critical pretending to help pretending to want you to do
your very best which this latest isn't quite and so what if you
publish it in some glossy venue it won't pay the rent it won't even
pay for the software you bought because you hoped it might make
your too-mysterious digitations more like office work and now
that you've met the woman of your day-dreams who is a stripper
and lives up the street with a baby named michael I hope you
won't go spoil it all by writing a poem

OUT OF THE SILENCE

THE POEM THAT ARRIVES OUT OF

Only the deaf know silence.
And because they have nothing else
to compare it with, they cannot elaborate
its theoretical characteristics. The poem
out of silence is a gesture of infinite
futility, attractive because it won't
let us conclude. It can only be written
with words we agree not to speak
even to ourselves, even in the dark
spiced privileged air
of the Catholic confessional.

Speech after long silence is not
only right, it is better
than speech after lots of talk.
Vive la différence! The question
is   not
how silence means but that
it helps to keep distinct hundreds
of billions of words. Think
of a sentence without blank space.
In the Thai language (on the page,
even on billboards in public places)
there are nospacesbetweenwords
because they have understood that
oncewestartwedon'tstopuntilwe
emptyournarrativedesireforjustaveryshort
breath. Thenwebeginanewutterancewhichgoeson
quitehappilysinuousasalovelysnakeofsense.

Out of silence only silence comes.
In its soft, white, slightly soiled
clothes. Hoping
against its own timeless evidence
to be redeemed forever by one intense conversation,
or at least temporarily by shouts
of anger, angst, beatitude, accusation: the chaos
we pretend to clarify with public uproar.
Yet we maintain that silence
is what we need
to get back to, our cool
bodies draped in see-through negligence
or the limitless grace of an indifferent
syntax. We'd really like to shut
up. But we can't. We know that if we stopped
scrolling for even a minute the stupidity
of our systems would collapse around us.
We understand the value of silence.
We always invite it to preside at our
inquiries into the nature of meaning itself.
We regale it with conundrums about how we could not
reason (in all honesty) without at least the least
idea of it. But when it comes home, exhausted
and beautiful, sexy, naked and pure beyond belief, we
do not rub its back and put it to bed. We
blame it and praise it and make it the first cause
of words we release only when they've agreed
to forget their life in the blood, their brief
epiphanies, their devout preparations,
their residence in the bone harp of the throat.

Writing a poem out of silence is like typing
on a computer that erases the last word
whenever you hit the space bar. If you seek
to discover the most advanced virtual experience
of silence for yourself, there it is.

126

Thumb it.   See?

And the only glitch might be
the noise the keyboard makes
while it records, invisibly,
and without conscience,
everything which can be seen
to un-occur for as long as

a Dallas Cow
Girl with long blonde
legs executes
a slow
roll
in a prison of blue
water: bubbles
rise from her hair

a model
train from the era
of robber barons
chugs, the choo-choo
puffing around
a figure eight track
on a table in a penthouse
under a triple-paned
window in which the city
works itself up
like an architect's
vision of industrial
inevitability, smoking
and swarming, erasing
most of the sky

a dolphin leaps
into freeze frame

male dancers in puce
tights, their upper
bodies oiled and hard
as breastplates, whirling
in unison, eating

chunks of sponge
cake the colour
of cooled lava

a black Mercedes, cruising
New Mexico, windows
dotted with slow
clouds

a glassy sky
scraper shakes
in the wind, leaking
wisps of chartreuse gas

the sea
black
and patchy
as the skin
of a dead
whale

white light
so
full of it
self
it evaporates
thoughts
of tomorrow

FOR JIDDU KRISHNAMURTI

"Do what is easy.
Do what you love to do."

So simple. But how *can* we
give up our addiction
to struggle and alarm? We understand
that the blunt abutments of thought
can dissolve into grace,
into silence, and yet
we can't seem to leave the gym
we've made out of glamour and the spit
shine of work.
                    Listen,
let what goes on forever sing
through the tiniest cul-de-sac you thought
you could hide in. A shuddering
lightness and the body's war
is gone. Every split second
takes it further away and we
go on with what we were doing,
awake now, and groundlessly happy.

Above the black-boned
        hanging lamp's
            river misted
                hills in milky glass
            large petals
        of light float
    on the ceiling, turning
        and re-turning above
            the slow sea
                murmur of mixed
            vernaculars, the steamy ghosts
    of soup, the candle flame's
            shadow that billows and shrinks
                in the wall's red brocade
                    like the sleepy wings of a dragon
                this work day evening
            at The Wu Li
            and I look
            back over an afternoon
    full of words
        how the pencil creaked
            as it turned, how the blade
                skimmed off a ribbon
                    of rosewood edged in white
                which broke as it fell
                    into small fans

In the beginning there was always
(though we left it like a shed
skin to dry at the back of the cave
of the mind) the need to know
what went on before us.

Believing what we took
for memories we began
to obey imperatives: Fate,
Gods, Biology, dream work, stories
about the star at the core
of an apple, the sweet
flare of light in animal eyes.

> *To begin is to enter always*
> *days that have already come*
> *to pass: visions*
> *eaten without salt by fanatics,*
> *milestones, codes, epiphanies:*
> *collapsed stars in the mind . . .*

When mayflies tumble out of the sun
to litter the sidewalks and pavements
of lakeside resorts;
when comets with tighter schedules
than buses or trains
return from the limitless night
we lived in before we learned
how to scratch
pictures on the walls
of caves; insights
flash through a husk
of selves and the light

they admit reveals
as it fades
a shadow dance
a slipped encounter soft as rain.

MISERICORDIA GENERAL

for Robert Emmet Finnegan

The window
itself can't change
and I can't move
enough to change
what it shows me:
the soiled brick
wall, part of a white
windowframe,
four telephone wires:
consciousness distilled
to the space between
this tireless machine that breathes
for me, and a block
of sheltered lives.

   The swamp invades
   itself   Under scum
   and broad pads   green
   jaws cruise   Almost
   nothing
   remembers how
   to breathe

   Slippery tongs
   grip   Suddenly

   flesh gives way

     A long, slow
      slide and I'm

        there

My lungs fill and burn

Grand Prairie. I was born
here. Cannonades
of light over the snow
left me hungry for exotic
wars.
                Hard
to believe, after years
in the signal corps,
the great pyramid
cells, the horns
of grey matter, anterior
columns and tracts blown
like power-lines and bridges . . .

Only my eyes move.

At first they brought me
books, turned
pages till I slept.
I blinked messages
like radio code into deep
space. Nothing
got through. I learned
to concentrate on the view.

Today the wall has broken
out in a cold sweat
as though it were ill,
as though the whole damn world . . .

But no. By noon
the bricks are dry.
By dusk they're warm and snug.

I'm lying on a bed
of brick that stretches
and curves to the round
horizon   The sky
is a glass kiln   Hot
wind mixed with green
shadow dyes
my hospital gown dark
as a forest   The bricks
glow   Thick
smoke all around
me then the gown bursts
into flame   Ashes
float   I can't
feel a thing but waves
that melt in the air make
my eyes water and open

to darkness that thins
as the wall returns . . .

Of course it's not just
a wall; it's earth, pulverized
rock, shaped
by fire and sweat – lore
old as the Chaldees.

                     I remember
the mason I worked for once
(the exact mouth, face
baked like a mask of the desert
under a shock of white
hair, the spare
frame, crooked fingers,
eyes bright as a hawk's)

digging his loam in October
letting it powder under the frost
mixing the weathered remains with spring
water, ground chalk, ashes
bone meal, coal dust, or dried
seeds pounded to grist, tempering this
to a smooth pug with his feet
culling and kneading each clot
lifting it over his head
slamming it down into the slick
or sanded beechwood mould and stockboard,
squaring the top with a wet strike,

lugging the raw brick on pallets
up to the drying ground,
laying them in a scintle hack
under straw to cure in the air,

stacking up codes in a kiln
he knew he'd have to break
and build and break and build
again, every three years,

kindling the fire holes
with twigs and paper
"to drive off water smoke,"
raising the heat with stove logs,
then charcoal.
                        Seal the arches,
let it cook for a week.

I'd help him draw the cooled stock,
astonished at the way some change
in temper, heat, or stack pattern
could produce shades
of red from scarlet to blood

pudding, pinks, browns, ochre, sulphur,
buff, orange, and grey
to green or woodsmoke blue.

And they weren't just bricks, but phrases
of a composition he kept
in his head, some chimney, garden walk
or fireplace or gateway
and maybe, if the client could pay,
a glazed puzzle that would resolve
itself into emblems, a coat
of arms, a dignified profile, scenes
from daily life.
                    He worked
all over the world, and worked on the day
he died at ninety-four: single
withe, cavity walls, header
and stretcher, spreading the beds,
furrowing and parging, buttering ends,
keeping the plumb line straight
to the rim of the course,
raking or beading or tuck pointing.

English bond, Flemish bond,
running bond, and cross bond,
garden wall and herringbone and Sussex
noggings and surrounds,
pillars, arches, and quoins
(I studied this, there
in the war) strapwork,
gaugework, dentil sets
and rusticated patterns.

Out in the high sun
finishing a patio or pool, tap tap
tap, and the brick, fieldstone,

flagstone, tile, would crack
a perfect closer.

    Night   The siren
    gives up its pewter
    ghost   Time
    is a glass shock
    wave that evaporates
    nerve ends   *The first*
    mortar explodes
    the dark like a brimstone
    flower   I'm over
    the hill at last but the same
    habits cry
    the dragon back
    from her peace   Reeds
    now, hollow
    music. Whatever
    it touches bleeds. "I'm flying
    without support ahead
    of the storm   There are no
    thresholds   Everything
    is now"
        This
    is what we were taught
    to fear, this play
    of self in the snow
    taste of remembered
    mornings, in the long
    dark, empty of almost
    anyone else, but it
    sings, this way
    of touching the near
    silence where all
    the mind can reach
    and become and allow

to fade fills
even a desolate
street with spring
light that slowly
explodes my cropped
view of the world

From the top right-hand
corner, telephone lines
like an empty musical
staff drape down
and away

 electron streams
 vowels and voice
 colours blurred
 to a hum

where birds come
to rest. Somewhere
they have nests and futures.

This time
it's a grackle, ugly
eyes, feathers glistening
like Texas crude, the beak
opens and I hear, inside,
the sound of a stone
breaking, like the cracked note
of the bugle that played taps
at Arlington for J. F. K.

Life has these necessary
flaws that say don't
gloat, each triumph
is shadowed by invisible failures,

all of them real, though disguised
by ritual observance.

Sunfoil flashes
Aerosol   Aerosol   Aerosol

Backpacks and party girls
Police out on the roads

Courage, old heart.
Somewhere in this
paradigm, the lion sleeps.

I had lost count
of the days, the nights, jars
of glucose hung like sterilized
fruit. Could I have
known how immeasurable
sleep would be
redeemed by bricks? Like faces
in a stadium they look
the same but have their own
wrinkles and weather
marks, the white
stain of efflorescence,
some of them edged
by years of soot
to formal death
letters – diverse
histories, none
of them perfectly true.

Cockle shells
Cockle shells

To warm the heart?
No. The sea
after all
is cold. Deep
fissures in a
thunderhead. I should
have been that.

Sometimes (in dreams?
I can't always recognize
that shift out of every
-day) bricks
burn and pulse like blood
cells, their ember
flare darkening
at dusk when part
of the windowframe ignites
and glows, yellow
through soft curtains.

I have imagined
a woman in that room, singing
her name to myself,
watching her intelligent eyes
in conversation. Soon, we will touch.
Our skins will heat and cool in the dark.
There will be children
and friends whose lives
bind ours to the world.

    (I know that's not true
    or perfect. I know the film
    that keeps insight
    from outlook, but why
    should I care? Death
    itself can only hurt

as much as a drawn
shade. I've got
what many say
they want:

> no worries, no pain
> no one to fight with
> no one to blame
> and nothing left
> to account for.)

Though I can't see
the sun, I can watch
its moods, modes,
and seasons, the day
changing – fierce or soft
with mist – rain, leaves
loose in the wind, shadows
of smoke opening, a gull's
keen glide, the snow
arriving, straight
or swirled, ice
that shines and runs.

> *A white horse gallops*
> *across the field*
> *into a still*
> *cloud, and the west*
> *blue rings like an anvil.*

Here, there is time
to dream a new life
before death, before
the 'copters bursting in air,
the sudden drill
of pain in my head,
the mud, the lasting silence.

Most of the poems in this collection were first published in the following books, anthologies, journals, and periodicals:

Alpha Beat Soup; *Arc*; *Bogg*; *Cokefish*; *Black Apple*; *Border Crossings*; *CVII*; *Canada Poetry Review*; *Canadian Literature*; *Caprice*; *Descant*; *Garden Varieties* (Cormorant, 1988); *Ideas of Shelter* (Turnstone, 1981); *Inscriptions* (Turnstone, 1992); *The Lyric Paragraph: Canadian Prose Poems* (DC Books, 1987); *Manitoba Writers' News*; *Margin*; *More Garden Varieties* (Aya Press, 1989); *More Garden Varieties Two* (The Mercury Press, 1990); *The New Quarterly*; *NeWest Review*; *Nimrod*; *Other Voices*; *Out of Place: Stories and Poems* (Coteau, 1991); *Pittsburgh Quarterly*; *Pivot*; *Poetry Australia*; *Poets On: Remembrance*; *Poets' Gallery*; *Prairie Fire*; *Prism International*; *Raffia*; *Saturday Night*; *Secrets from the Orange Couch*; *Towards 2000: Poems for the Future* (Fifth House, 1991); *Underpass*; *Vintage 92* (Sono Nis, 1993); and *Waves*.

Italic passages in "A *Splintered Garland for the Seer*" are from Hart Crane, *The Complete Poems and Selected Letters and Prose*, Brom Weber, ed., Liveright, 1966.

I would like to thank David Arnason, Lorna Crozier, Jim Keller, Robert Kroetsch, Patrick Lane, and Kevin Roberts for their advice and support; Mhari Mackintosh, whose close reading and detailed notes on earlier draughts were invaluable; and Stan Dragland, Poetry Editor at McClelland and Stewart, whose astute suggestions coaxed the book into its present form.